CHRISTIAN THINKING ABOUT
INDUSTRIAL LIFE

Christian Thinking
about
Industrial Life

George Wilkie

THE SAINT ANDREW PRESS
EDINBURGH

First published in 1980 by
THE SAINT ANDREW PRESS
121 George Street, Edinburgh EH2 4YN

Copyright © G. D. Wilkie 1980

ISBN 0 7152 0449 1

Printed in Great Britain by Bell and Bain Ltd.

Contents

Introduction

This document started off life as a Report to a Committee and still bears many of the hallmarks of its origin. It was, however, an attempt not merely to record what is being done but rather where we have got to in our thinking. And since there is little available in print on this subject, it was thought that it might interest a wider readership. Indeed, in putting it together I have had in mind part-time industrial chaplains and Christian laymen in industry, who might find such a collation useful.

I should stress that it is a gathering together of thoughts and ideas from many and varied sources. To a large extent it is a scissors and paste job – selecting bits and pieces written or collected over the years – and it is personal only in the sense that I have not obtained the approval of others for the statements it contains.

Many of the ideas, however, are in no sense original and have long been common currency in Industrial Mission circles. In a few cases where I can remember the origin of an idea I have acknowledged it. Otherwise I'm relying on the tolerance of my colleagues – both laymen and chaplains.

It was R. H. Tawney who said, 'Political principles resemble military tactics; they are usually designed for a war that is over'. In a like way it may be felt that much of what this Report contains applies to industry as it was rather than as it is.

Certainly there are a number of big new developments coming up over the horizon which aren't seriously touched on here – not least the question marks over the place of work in human life in future and the social implications of what has been called 'de-industrialisation'. We so often struggle to get 'alongside' industry as we know it, only to discover that it has moved away from us and faces new challenges!

The absence of any serious discussion of these issues here should not be taken to mean that industrial missioners have not got them in their sights or that they are not already wrestling with them. It seemed worthwhile, however, to record some of the insights gained so far, in the hope that we may feel freer to cope with the new issues which confront us in industrial society today.

G.D.W.

Part I

Why the Church in Industry?

In 1926 – the year of the General Strike – the reports to the General Assembly of the Church of Scotland contained no reference to the industrial unrest which was affecting the lives of millions of people at that time.

This does not mean that Christians were unconcerned. But it does remind us of the generally accepted view of previous generations that the Church's job is to see the word faithfully preached on Sunday and not to 'interfere' with the world of men's work. It is up to the layman to apply Christian principles in secular situations.

There is an important principle here which our Scottish Church has always upheld – that each individual Christian should have personal responsibility (and freedom) to act as he thinks best. And one of the humbling features of visiting industrial works is the number of Christians one meets whose courageous witness is acknowledged by all. It would be false to underestimate the effect on the Scottish nation of the faithful preaching of the Word over the years.

Bewilderment

But there is also evidence among men in high and low places in industry of a degree of bewilderment and despair in knowing how to relate the 'word' given on Sunday to the complex situations they find themselves in during the week.

When I announced to my first Kirk Session on Clydeside (shipyard workers to a man) that I intended to visit a local shipyard as an industrial chaplain, they told me, 'You're wasting your time. You can't be a Christian in a shipyard'. They were the most loyal elders you could wish for, prepared to sacrifice time and energy for 'Church' work. But they couldn't marry Church and yard.

Their hold on their job was always tenuous, and too often they found themselves under compulsion to accept practices which seemed contrary to Christian teaching; to go with the majority in decisions which enshrined half-truths; and sometimes to survive only at the expense of another man whose need was as great as their own. These men represent many others over the years who have wanted to see 'righteousness prevail', but who have found that, in industrial life, principles can get impossibly bent and compromised.

Not good enough

In this situation it is not good enough for the Church to go on propounding principles when honest men feel defeated in attempting to work them out in their lives. A caring Church will move out to where men are exposed to such circumstances in an effort to come alongside them with understanding and sympathy. The arm of the Church must not be so shortened that it cannot share with men their problems and dilemmas until new understandings of the Christian Faith emerge which take account of the realities of industrial life, and to which men can enthusiastically commit themselves.

This is the task of the Church in industry. It is a joint effort of ministers and laymen. Its agenda is industrial life, and its aim is to bring all of it to the touchstone of Jesus Christ.

Teachings and structures

How do we come to be in this situation? Part of the problem relates to the Church's teaching and the difficulty of presenting it in a way which is relevant to the situations men face in industrial life. The New Testament's teaching is given against a background of a rural/agricultural society and often becomes distorted when applied 'direct' to industrial life. In particular it leaves men to face complex collective situations armed only with a personal ethic. (This is dealt with more fully in Part II.)

Similarly, patterns of Church life developed in an agriculturally-based society have been given an 'everlasting' aura which properly belongs only to the Gospel and this has weakened the Church's ability to respond to changing social patterns. Satisfaction with things 'as they always have been' (though they haven't) has weighed heavily against the search for more appropriate forms of Church life to match the changed circumstances of men's working life. One of the pioneers of industrial mission, Bishop Ted Wickham, has said, 'The Church is not a rock standing in the middle of the stream of life, impervious to the waters swirling around it. It is a strong current in the stream, influencing and directing its character and course in all the changing circumstances of its journey'.

Industrial Revolution

It is our contention that something happened at the Industrial Revolution which radically changed the life of the ordinary man in our society, and that the significance of this change has hardly yet been appreciated by the Churches. Canon Cardign, one of the early leaders of the Catholic Workers' Movement on the Continent, has declared, 'You can divide history into two main periods: From Abraham till James Watt; and from James Watt till the present day'. If, therefore, we aim to engage with men at the point of their working lives we must begin by trying to understand what happened as we changed from being a rural society to being an industrial society and how it affected ordinary people. And in order to be specific let us look, for instance, at the change which took place in the life of a weaver.

Weaver

In pre-industrial society the weaver was usually a man with a loom in a small back room. He was part of the domestic scene. The house was still the centre of his life and his family would help him as need arose. His working hours could be flexible and if there was not enough work for him at any particular time he could help someone else in the community. He might also train his son or another boy as a weaver and there was little capital needed, basically only a loom.

When the Industrial Revolution came, however, there was now power to drive a hundred looms at once and therefore they required a special place to house them – a manufactory. And thus *work became separated from the domestic scene* and the machine began to call the tune in man's life. There had now to be strict hours of work, man had to be there when the machine was working.

Far-reaching changes

1. There was a change in the *nature of work* itself – each man having only a small part to do. The weaver, for instance, might be employed in spinning or dyeing or weaving or despatching or designing, etc. For many workers there was less craft in the job and more machine minding. Also the worker didn't now know the man who supplied the raw materials. Nor did he know the customer for whom he was making the cloth. He was not really personally involved in the total job as he had been. His interest lay in his wages.

2. Another feature of the post-industrial society was the development of *collective relationships*. With hundreds and thousands of men employed in one factory they couldn't all have a personal relationship with 'the boss'. And so collective relationships developed. Pay and conditions of work were now negotiated as a body through a representative, and a man became one voice among hundreds.

3. With the development of industrial society there arose a *new class structure* (not that there hadn't always been class divisions but there was now a new basis for them). Capital was now needed if a man was to get employment (not just a few tools plus his skill). This led to a division between the owners of capital (buildings, equipment,

machinery, etc.) and those who had only their labour to offer. Thus, whereas a pre-industrial apprentice expected to be as his master one day, after the Industrial Revolution he expected to become a journeyman or at best a foreman. Someone who was going to be a master entered the industrial arena at a different level. This led to segregation and division not only within industry but in society also, with separate education, separate housing, etc. The result of this was that people in different classes were not likely to meet each other or even see each other, and this could lead to all sorts of misunderstandings and prejudices.

4. Another feature of the new industrial society was the possibility of *mass unemployment*. Whereas previously if there was no work a weaver could get a job in the community helping someone else, now when there was unemployment hundreds and thousands of men were out of work and could not be absorbed by the rest of the community. The fact that their work was tied to export markets and subject to the vagaries of world trade meant that life became very uncertain. This bred an attitude of 'live for the day' and also 'stand by one another in times of difficulty'.

5. As a result of these factors the work area of men's lives became an area of *uncertainty and conflict*. It was a world of big powers and forces over which the individual worker had no control – financial powers, technological powers, international powers, trade cycles, etc. These could either make or break him and they were in other people's hands. His life could be changed overnight and that affected the way he looked at the future.

Struggle

So why did these Port Glasgow elders say, 'You can't be a Christian in a shipyard?' I think basically because daily work for them was a struggle – not just a physical struggle to do it but a struggle to hold your place – a struggle which at times demanded fairly brutal tactics – a struggle for survival – a struggle in which military terms like 'the strike weapon' were used, etc. And so men of the highest ideals found themselves involved in things which didn't seem to square with these ideals.

The general assumption was that you *had* to accept the standards of industry. So I suppose that the idea that I might come amongst them was a threat to the uneasy compromise of their lives. Anyway they had been brought up to understand that the job of the Church was to build up its own life and not meddle in the affairs of industry.

Differing ethics

One further feature of working life which is important for us in the Church to grasp is the contrast between the middle class ethic and that of the working class.

The *middle class* ethic is individualistic and concerned with personal uprightness. Advance in working life depends upon the person himself and he expects increasing rewards for a large part of his life. He takes personal decisions. He is willing to look to the future and accept low rewards to begin with in the hope of better things in the future. His struggle is against other individuals on the way up the ladder – though this struggle is conducted in an honourable way. Society seems to be organised to allow for this personal advance.

The *working class* ethic is more group oriented. A man is a member of a group and any increase in his reward usually depends on the whole group getting it. He often has his top wage at the age of 21 and he is not looking to the future in the same way as the middle class youth. The uncertainty of life affects his attitude to saving and his hesitation about taking on long-term commitments. His situation inculcates the spirit of loyalty to other workers rather than striving against them for advancement, and society seems to be organised so that he doesn't have as much power and influence.

Out of date?

It may be said that a lot of this description of the situation is out of date and things have changed over the last two centuries. And it must be confessed that the 'wind of change' has affected, and is affecting, industrial life as other areas of life. There would have to be many modifications in this statement if it were to describe the situation as it is today. In particular the advent of the microprocessor (the chip) is having a profound effect on industrial and commercial life, leading to what some would describe as the Second Industrial Revolution.

But it is important that we note what happened at the first industrial revolution which set in motion the process which has produced our present situation. The main thing to be emphasised is the move on the part of the great majority away from attitudes and experiences of rural society. Far too many of the assumptions implicit in the Church's present structures and teaching still relate to conditions of life in pre-industrial society.

Our claim is that the Church today needs to know men in the context of their working environment if the Gospel is to be taken seriously. The Church will not recognise the working identity of a man unless it is in some sense present within the work situation. It would be far easier if a man's whole life was spent in one community served by a neighbourhood Church – as it was in the pre-industrial days. But the 'facts of life' today are not so simple. Men live in a number of different communities and the Church must be ready to adjust its ways to meet changing conditions.

For example

Other organisations have met with the same problem. Trade unions, for instance, in the early days were organised mainly in branches based on a man's home neighbourhood. And in many trade unions this is still the basis of the official organisation. Today, few men attend their branch meetings – and they would not know many of their fellow-members if they did. They haven't so much in common.

But there has been an upsurge of trade union activity on the factory floor – the place where men meet daily and have common interests. The shop steward has taken a more important place in the work of the union in negotiating and bargaining and, in some places, the convener of shop stewards is a full-time official paid by the firm. Both workers and management realise that it is within the works community that real decisions are taken and attitudes developed, rather than at branch level.

Is there not a lesson for the Church here? Although the local congregation is a vital part of the Church's organisation, it is not the only place where the Church must exist today. As so many of the activities of men have moved out of the residential parish, the Church must go with them. Otherwise it will limp along in a truncated form because it is no longer in touch with a major part of the lives of men.

No buildings

But how can the Church exist in industry? The so-called 'industrial community' has no exact geographical location. It's a network of relationships rather than a place. And factories are places where men work, not where they have time for services or meetings or normal 'church' activities. Further, the Church in industry must not attempt to be just another industrial pressure group, which would only make the confusion worse.

Perhaps the fact that the 'normal' structures of the Church do not fit this situation is not a bad thing as it forces us to think again about the meaning and purpose of the Church and how it can exist in a changing world. Not having buildings, at least reminds us that the Church exists in the world through people.

Jesus saw his disciples as both 'leaven' and a 'light' in the world. How then do we support and resource the people who are the Church in the industrial world for their role as leaven? And how do we present the light of the Gospel in industry today? The life of the home-based congregation will have its place but it needs to be supplemented by a Church presence nearer the places where people work.

The advent of chaplains

At this point is is impossible not to refer to the growth of the industrial chaplaincy movement, both because of what it is in its own right and for the effect it has had on the general movement of industrial mission. Its beginnings during and after the second world war were, to say the least, informal and perhaps even accidental. However, it was soon taken within the formal structure of the Church and has been widely accepted in Scottish industry.

There is considerable vagueness both in Church and industry about what it is all about. It is a tribute to our forefathers that it is not considered wholly unnatural that ministers should be found alongside men at their daily work. From industry's point of view (and chaplains are not appointed without approval of both men and management) the chaplain's role can be considered in terms of the service he can offer to employees. From the chaplain's point of view, access to a place of work gives him an opportunity of meeting and thinking with men about the whole spectrum of human activity in the context of their work experience.

Although the minister or priest (it is an ecumenical effort) is not the Church, yet his presence in industry does convey the message that the Church cares about this area of human life also.

And apart from the general service he has to offer, the chaplain's presence has been seen as a support to Christians in their working life. (For a fuller description of the work of chaplains see 'Industrial Chaplain's Manual'.)

Full-time chaplains

In 1962 the Church of Scotland appointed its first full-time industrial chaplain in Greenock/Port Glasgow. The need for such an appointment arose because of a widespread feeling among part-time chaplains that the Church was only scratching at the surface of the problem and that the opportunities were limitless. A full-time chaplain would not only be able to visit more widely than part-time chaplains but would be able to engage in more depth in discussion about the character and quality of industrial life – and to reflect on the theology related to it.

Since 1963, four other full-time chaplains have been appointed, serving in major industrial centres. Both locally and as a national team they have been attempting to represent the Church and the Church's thinking in an informed way within the industrial community. They have also engaged in what might be called 'service' to industry in the fields of alcoholism, redundancies, industrial relations, training programmes, etc. And they have developed a network of contacts with people at all levels of industry.

And committed laymen

One result of their activities has been the emergence of a body of laymen who are, to a greater or lesser degree, committed to the Christian way in industry and who meet from time to time in local or national groups on an explicitly Christian basis.

There is almost total absence of formal organisation of such laymen. Their names may only be recorded in the memory of an industrial chaplain – or perhaps on a list of people who attended a previous meeting. They come together because of concern about some issue, or for mutual support in daily industrial living. They have found the activities sponsored by chaplains supportive in their working lives and they, more than any other group, are keen that there should be a Church presence in the industrial world.

Twin groupings

At present, therefore, the Church's work in industry is based on the twin groupings of industrial chaplains and committed laymen. These form a loose network scattered throughout Scottish industry which is referred to as 'industrial mission'. There has always been a great reluctance to have any more formal organisation than is absolutely necessary. And although we appreciate that operating without formal structures is only possible because of the support of the Church's own structures, nevertheless we feel that at this stage the informal approach is the right one in industry.

It may be that in future some more definite organisation will be required in order to facilitate the work. If so, it is to be hoped that it will be allowed to emerge from the needs of the situation and flexible enough to change as the world changes.

Parish role

It is not to be expected that great numbers of men in industry will see their Christian witness in relation to such a committed group, however. For most, the local congregation will be the primary place where they will find resources for their life in the working world. An important part of industrial mission therefore must take place within the parish; through feeding-in any new understanding of the Faith gained in the workplace; through briefing sessions for ministers and students, including industrial visits and interviews; through support for congregational groups where people can share their working experience with others; through training programmes for the young and through existing adult organisations. The local congregation too, can be a place of real meeting where people from differing work situations listen to each other and try to look at things from the other person's point of view, so that myths can be challenged and understanding built up.

Integrating force

It is not the aim of industrial mission 'to bring the divisions of society into the Church'. Our fear is that if by our Church organisation we concentrate on the domestic and local scene, one vital part of the life of man – his work experience – can easily be left out, so that (like the Port Glasgow elders) he is left to cope with an unwholesome divisiveness in his own life. If the Christian Faith is to be the integrating force it can be in our society, the experience of men and women at work must take its place alongside their experience in families and local communities as being the focus of our Gospel and the context in which we discover the Faith for our day.

Part II

Insights for Christians
in Industry

Introduction

The response of the Church to the difficulties of
men in industry, however, must not only be in terms
of chaplains and structures. If, as we have claimed,
part of the problem is that men have been unable to
relate the Church's teaching to real-life situations,
then we must ask what new insights have emerged
from the Church's approach so far. In the main,
such new understanding as has arisen has come in
the course of the discussion of actual working
situations rather than from 'applying' basic rules or
doctrines (although occasionally some neglected
doctrine appears in an exciting new light when held
alongside industrial life).

This approach is known as the '*inductive method*'
which starts from the world and from human
experience and seeks to discover the meaning of the
Faith in relation to them. In the context of 'doing
theology', Dr. Ramsey, a past Archbishop of
Canterbury, has said: 'The Inductive method doesn't
start with the word 'God' or the concept of 'God'. It
starts with people as they are and thinks with them
about life having meaning and purpose. It points to
things which have an imperative about them – love,
self-sacrifice, courage, etc. As a result of this, men
begin to discover there is something within them
and about them which is part of them and yet

24

beyond them. In a word, the 'absolutes' – and these absolutes are shared with others. Putting them all together gives you something that makes sense of society and the universe.

'In such a discussion the person of Jesus Christ is legitimately brought on to the scene, partly because he is the embodiment of the things we have been talking about and partly because he is greater than them. We get a foretaste of the inductive method in the parables of Jesus, very often with questions at the end, e.g. the parable of the vineyard.'

In the context of industrial mission, the inductive method means exploring with those involved, actual situations from their daily experience, holding Christian teaching alongside them, and trying to discover biblical themes, which will shed light on these situations and help the participants to respond more positively and confidently.

Fragmentary

Such understanding of the Christian Faith as emerges from this inductive process is not strong on definitions or dogmas – still less does it produce a comprehensive re-statement of the Faith. It tends to be fragmentary and unstructured and consist of insights and clues about human living. It encourages an approach to life in terms of what J. H. Oldham used to call, 'A Dialogue with God', rather than the mechanical application of pre-determined 'principles'.

Any attempt, therefore, to present in a systematic way some of the ideas that have emerged from our discussions is bound to falsify the truth to a greater or lesser degree – if not to deny the validity of the whole process by which we arrive at it. Yet enlightenment is taking place and certain themes recur frequently enough to become part of our common understanding and therefore worth passing on. As a compromise I have chosen eight general headings and tried to record what has seemed to me most important under one or other of them. The result is, to say the least, fragmentary but may spark off further thought and discussion, leading to deeper insights, appropriate to working life today.

Indeed, one reason for making this collection is to help us to see where we have got to so far, so that we can face the continually changing scene with a clearer vision and find the *new* insights which will be needed for the decade ahead.

FACING THE TRUTH

The following quotes, overheard in group discussion, suggest the way our thinking is developing.

(a) 'What can Christians bring to the debate about the future of our society? Basically, we hope, *a passion to seek the truth*, or at least to seek explanations which are not over-simplified, or too complex, or based on doctrine. Sometimes a willingness to accept the truth that we do not know everything and that we would be better to proceed in faith, acknowledging our ignorance, than accept glib explanations from whatever quarter they come.'

(b) 'Beware the *snap-shot view* which seldom represents the truth'. This is a view of an industrial situation at one moment in time (usually a moment of crisis) and from one perspective, taking no

account of what has gone before or of wider
considerations which must affect the truth (for
instance ignoring the emotional problems involved
in accepting change; impatience with the 'ritual
dance' which usually accompanies wage
negotiations; applying personal ethics to collective
situations; assuming 'middle-class' ambitions for
working-class people, etc.). Those whom Jesus
rebuked for their criticism of Mary's generous use of
her box of ointment suffered from a similar limited
vision.

(c) 'Beware the *quick fix-it*'. Too many people
believe that it exists and there is never a shortage of
those who are ready to offer a formula for it. But it
is not true to experience and when applied usually
leads to other problems which had not been
foreseen (what the French call 'problematique'). As
one managing director said, 'Don't come here with
"solutions" to my problems. They'll almost certainly
be wrong. But if you can give me a little bit of
insight that will help me to take the next step more
confidently, I'll be grateful.' When the disciples
failed to find a quick cure for the epileptic boy Jesus
said, 'This kind cometh not out, but by prayer and
fasting'. Not less is required for the ills of the
industrial world.

(d) 'Beware the man with a "*total solution*"'.
Those who offer comprehensive blueprints for the
solution of industrial and social problems have
seldom reckoned with the limitations of man and
the complexities of life. Inevitably the rigorous
application of such solutions leads to the
manipulation of man in the interests of the 'final
solution'. The Kingdom of God which Christians

seek, while demanding serious social concern, is always 'provisional' in this world. It is also always the 'alternative society' in any society – even Christendom.

(e) 'Beware the *idols* which men have erected in the market place' (cf. Cordingley). The world hasn't noticed that, as the secularisation process has proceeded and as the Christian God has been progressively removed from the market place, other gods have been created to watch over the destinies of men and to command their allegiance – such things as 'Economic Growth', 'Free Collective Bargaining', 'The Classless Society', 'Profitability' – even 'Full Employment'. There's a lot of truth in all of these and they have inspired men to work for a better society. The danger is that we give them ultimate significance and bend everything to meet their requirements.

The story of the Israelites with their golden calf is full of significance in relation to the 'sacred cows' of modern society. When men abolish God from their midst, they still find it necessary to make other gods on which they can pin their faith. Whatever else faith in the Christian God does, it allows us to keep the proximate things of this world in their place.

(f) We must recognise the *myths about each other* with which we live. After a recent conference one participant wrote, 'What struck me most forcibly, as it has done on other occasions, was the degree to which mistrust stems from mutual ignorance on the part of the principal groups (in industry). Management knows the facts of its own situation but does not know much about the main concerns of the trade union people and believes a certain mythology about the shop-floor situation. The unions know the facts about their situation and cherish an even more distorted view of the position of managements. The fact is that there is remarkably little dialogue between the principal groups, so that the mythology remains unchallenged on both sides and, in fact, becomes more deeply entrenched.'

The writer went on to say that the gathering of people from all sections of industry, under the sponsorship of the Church, was one of the few opportunities he knew of for men to meet and listen and have their myths challenged. Christians will see this as an important part of 'facing the truth'.

But there may be an even deeper reason for bringing such people together. Jesus said, 'The Kingdom of God is among you'. It is there to be discovered whenever the barriers are lowered between Jews and Samaritans, Greeks and barbarians, managers and workers. Whenever they really listen to each other and think of the other's problems myths are corrected – but also, relationships are created which are of the stuff of the Kingdom.

(g) 'Our task is to help men *to enlarge their frame of reference*'. We tend to assess the actions and attitudes of others in terms of a rigid conceptual framework. Everything must be made either to fit within our frame of reference or else be ignored. The Marxist who – surrounded by some captains of industry – said, 'What worries me is that I can't find a real capitalist among you', was typical of all of us. His problem was that his frame of reference didn't allow for the possibility of the sort of capitalist he was meeting on this occasion. Jesus had this problem with the Jews, whose frame of reference didn't allow for the possibility of a 'good' Samaritan.

A Christian lives in expectancy of change, both in men and institutions, and he will be prepared to recognise it – and not be misled by labels which men apply (especially to themselves). He will also always be seeking to enlarge his own and other men's frames of reference, e.g. lengthening the time-scale of men's thinking; introducing the Third World dimension into considerations of justice; pointing to long-term aims and goals and working out short-term objectives in relation to them.

(h) 'Facing the Truth' means *recognising the presence of God everywhere in the life of the world.* Our frame of reference is one which allows for the activity of God in the words and deeds of men who make no formal commitment to him. It is easy for Christians to live with a 'closed-circuit view' which sees God only at work in Bible, Church or other confessing Christians. In the parable of the sheep and the goats Jesus makes it clear that this is not his world view. We have still to convince men that God is present in their ordinary conversation and that his Spirit moves among all men in the ordinary affairs of their lives.

PERSONAL

Of central concern for Christians must be the place and use of persons in industry. What happens to them? How do they act? How do they relate to each other? It would be impossible to do justice to this whole field in a report like this, but three points may give an idea of the direction of our thinking.

(a) *Alienation*. There is much written about the alienation of men in industry, partly because of the division of labour and partly the division between those who make decisions and those who obey. Marx was very concerned about this and expressed his concern in almost religious terms. The crime of industry was to deny masses of men the right to develop self-powers by denying them control over the shaping of the objects they produced. In industry the things men work with are alien to them. They have no real involvement in them and no responsibility for what is being created. The more efficient the system, the greater the alienation – and the greater the degradation of man.

There have of course been considerable changes since Marx wrote. But the element of alienation in industry is still a challenge to anyone concerned with the dignity of man. The task of Christians is not to call for unthinking acquiescence and obedience from workers, but both to encourage men to use what power they have in responsible decision-making and to point to ways in which they can have more such responsibility.

(b) *The importance of personal relationships*. In working life we come into contact with a lot of people *individually* – colleagues, superiors, supporting staff, as well as customers, suppliers, competitors, etc. With some of them we develop fairly close relationships. Jesus said the Kingdom of God was to be discovered in relationships between people. This is the place where the Kingdom will begin, if anywhere. So Christians stress the importance of taking personal relationships in industry seriously. 'What's happening in them?' 'What does our relationship mean to him/her?' 'What does it mean to me?' 'What does he expect from it?' 'What am I giving?'

The danger is that industry encourages me to see people only in terms of their function. 'Get me an electrician.' 'I need a labourer.' 'Send me a secretary.' It's possible to take the skill the person has to offer, to be closely involved with such a person in your daily work – and yet not to bother about the human being tied up with that skill. In other words, to use them – even to manipulate them for your own ends. Not to consider them as persons, with potential, with expectations, with needs and with rights.

It is, of course, important to respect the role of the other person – his function in the enterprise – but the Christian will stop and think of the person himself and the nature of his involvement with him *beyond* the functional relationship. If modern working conditions depersonalise people as it is alleged, Christians will be pushing the ball in the opposite direction by offering *real* relationships to their colleagues.

(c) *Don't forget the personal in disputes.* 'Sometimes in industry we get lost in its complexity. Industry is complex, technically and organisationally. But we can be led astray by attempting to get more and more sophisticated procedures for dealing with our problems. Sometimes you find people 'locked-in' in industrial situations, looking for the right formula to solve a problem which is really a problem between two individuals – two heads of department, two engineers who won't co-operate, manager and shop steward. We invent all sorts of organisational theories to explain the reason for the conflict. Perhaps what is needed is to get the two people concerned together and help them to face their personal conflict.' (Quote from group discussion.)

When you discover a simple human solution to what seemed a terribly complex problem, people feel a sense of liberation. There's a feeling that human beings can supersede the system. It's good for human relationships all round.

COLLECTIVE

The sheer size of many working units means we cannot have personal relationships with all. Yet we are involved with them and what we do affects their lives. Our relationship with them is through the collective group to which we belong, be it trade union, management team, skilled trade, profession, etc. This is the instrument for good or ill through which we must operate in developing good relationships with the wider circle of those with whom we are involved in our work. The individual's role is to take part in forming policies and attitudes which will determine relationships with others. Christians have many things to contribute in such groups – a passion for the truth, a willingness to admit mistakes, loyalty to colleagues, compassion for the underdog, acceptance of others' views, etc.

c

Not master

But such collective groups can raise questions for the Christian. He is not master of all that is done in his name and may not wholly agree with it. Groups are bound to emphasise self-interest. They exist for the good of their members. They talk about 'claims' and 'rights' – and even 'demands'. They move by majority decision.

Further, such groups exercise power and that is seldom wholly good or wholly evil – and either way someone may get hurt. So Christians may well feel uncomfortable in taking part in such activities. But they cannot opt out of collective relationships any more than they can opt out of personal relationships. It is within *both* that we are to discover the Kingdom of God.

If we are to succeed we must recognise and accept the differences between personal relationships and collective relationships. The former can be immediate and straightforward (however difficult!) The latter are slow and move towards their objectives by discussions and debates and resolutions and negotiations – and by many other devious routes. It is anything but immediate and straightforward and calls for a high degree of patience and persistence – and hope.

Christian contribution

One important contribution Christians have to make to such a group is in *keeping objectives clear*. There will almost certainly be many diverse motives and expectations (often unacknowledged) in the group. How necessary, therefore, for Christians to keep defining and re-defining objectives; reminding others of them; holding them alongside policies and programmes. Such an emphasis on maintaining objectives must always introduce the question of the ethical demands of whatever situation is being faced.

Perhaps, above all, Christians have to learn to make something *positive out of compromise.* It is not a word that Christians warm to. Yet in collective relationships the way forward is often by compromise – and it is not always a bad thing. It may be the means by which another step can be taken along the road to better relationships – allowing men to get on with the job and discover the 'better way' in the process. A Christian's attitude to compromise is important. It is not 'the best of a bad job'. It is a means to a better solution – and the Christian knows that the work towards that solution must go on.

Strange company

Christians involved in collective relationships may find themselves in 'strange' company and they must be prepared for misunderstanding and misrepresentation. Their objective must be the fulfilling of God's will rather than keeping their own hands clean. Jesus was not afraid to be associated with publicans and sinners.

The doctrine of justification by faith and not by works is relevant here. Too many Christians really believe in justification by works, which leads to the attitude that we must keep our hands clean and not get involved in anything that isn't absolutely 'pure'. The man who believes that he is totally unworthy anyway and dependent on God's grace for everything in life will be free to risk getting his hands dirty in the world for the cause of the Kingdom.

George Stewart, a deeply spiritual leader of a previous generation, used to say that just as it was no sin for the man out working in the world during the day to have dirty hands in the evening (it was more of a sin if they were still pure white!), so anyone who has really been 'in the world' with soul and spirit should not expect to remain clean.

HANDLING CONFLICT

Much has been said and written about conflict situations in industry and how to resolve them. And we should recognise how much has been achieved by the tireless efforts of men on all sides, committed to better industrial relations. But destructive conflicts still occur too frequently and eat away at the heart of the industrial community.

Any organisation, therefore, like the Christian church with its concern for 'brotherhood' and its reputation for 'reconciliation' might well be expected to bring special insights to bear in areas of industrial conflict. This may be so, but we must be careful not to give a false impression about what we have to offer or suggest that we have a bag of solutions waiting to be applied which will resolve all disputes.

When faced with a family dispute, Jesus refused a request for a 'just solution'. 'Who made me a judge or a divider amongst you', he said. His message was not to be confused with some magic formula which would produce 'solutions' to order, while leaving underlying causes untouched. His refusal to give a decision left the family to work it out for themselves. And so often it's in getting together to find a solution that conflict is resolved – rather than in knowing who's right and who's wrong.

Sign of health?

The fact that conflict exists is not always a bad thing. It can be a sign of health. It depends on what you do with it.

The Church too often gives the impression that it's out for 'peace at all costs' and thus becomes a defender of the status quo. This is not the Biblical view. Jesus said, 'I am come not to bring peace but a sword'. In many ages (including the first century), men were more aware of the revolutionary implications of Christianity than that it brought peace and quiet.

When there is conflict, it can mean that people on both sides are challenged to think again and find better ways. It can mean too that, in the larger sense, the quality of our society is good because men have freedom to voice conflicting views – to challenge and object.

Jesus' order

Nevertheless, healing conflict is of the utmost importance to Christians. Jesus said, 'If you have anything against your brother when you bring your gift to the altar, first go and be reconciled with your brother and then bring your gift'. *Reconciliation comes before worship.* That's a startling fact when you think of the importance the Church today gives to worship. But this is Jesus' order.

Christians are used to dealing with conflict between individuals and, needless to say, this is to be found in industrial life as elsewhere. Indeed, as has already been said, sometimes conflict which appears to be between two groups is in fact between two persons who are in positions of leadership. And it is important to recognise this.

In personal conflict situations a Christian begins by admitting his own faults and dealing with conflicts in himself which may be expressed in his behaviour towards others. This is what Jesus helped men to do. By his acceptance of them, they were able to accept themselves and therefore be free for new relationships with other people.

Groups also

This approach may be relevant to conflicts between groups also. It may be the task of the Christian firstly to ask, 'What in this group prevents reconciliation with the other group?' 'What in our attitude or behaviour or character prevents agreement with the other group?' This question is seldom asked in collective negotiations. The rights of one's own side are more frequently stressed. It may be the Christian's job to raise this self-questioning *within* the group. This is not being disloyal to his group but rather working for the long-term good of all.

But secondly, the resolution of conflict often involves hard bargaining in which differences between the two parties are faced squarely. In bargaining the aim is to discover areas of *agreement or common interest* between the two parties in conflict. This means:

   (i) clarifying the situation – identifying the real source of conflict.

  (ii) seeing what are the real issues at stake – especially getting the long-term picture into focus.

 (iii) discussing the basis on which a just settlement should be worked out.

 (iv) taking on negotiation of the agreement which is bound to be difficult and, to some extent, a compromise, but a compromise which everyone will work with.

Jesus said, 'Agree with your adversary before you go to the Judge', i.e. an *agreement worked out between parties* is much to be preferred to an imposed settlement by the law. Such an agreement has more chance of the willing support of both parties than one which they feel has been imposed upon them. This is why we in Britain prefer negotiated agreements (collective bargaining) freely entered into rather than bringing in the law to make the trade-unions or the management come into line.

Breakdown

There are times, of course, when negotiations break down and when the power which has so far been only a latent threat is brought out into the open. Withdrawal of labour is every man's right (strikes can only be outlawed in dictatorships), but such action is seldom undertaken with any great relish. Some short strikes are really 'procedural' –

undertaken to force the other side to have a meeting, for instance – but longer ones usually come when there is a deep gulf between the two sides which talking has failed to bridge.

Various Christian groups have listed the essential conditions for a 'just strike'. The points that usually appear in such lists are:

  (i) The strike must be just in itself when looked at in relation to the rest of society.

 (ii) Agreed procedures must have been worked through.

(iii) There must be proportion and balance in the action (no using a sledge-hammer to crack a nut).

(iv) The means used should be peaceful. There should be no violence in picketing, etc.

 (v) The harmful effect on others should be seriously considered.

Such lists can be no more than guides, however, and it is impossible to construct a check-list for those who want to make sure a strike is just. Situations and circumstances vary greatly.

A strike is not always a bad thing. It may be the only honest way to move forward and Christians may well find themselves accepting the responsibility of leadership. It may be the only way to demonstrate a depth of feeling which hasn't been taken seriously so far. It may serve a useful purpose in allowing parties to stand back and look at the whole scene. Or it may provide a necessary release for pent-up feelings, not only about matters in dispute but about other things which have caused discontent – and that can be a cleansing process.

But strikes can also be destructive – both in terms of personalities and of relationships. It is important, therefore, that the will towards agreement is maintained and clarified during the strike. There can be a tendency, at least initially, to adopt an 'all or nothing' approach which, if maintained, may cause unnecessary suffering. In such circumstances it may be difficult for reason to prevail. A Christian contribution will always keep in view the fact that both sides at some point have to work together again and that the aim is still to find an acceptable and workable compromise.

Beyond agreement

Finally we should remember that Christians are concerned not just with an agreement which may be accepted for varying reasons and may indeed be accepted under duress, or because it satisfies an immediate self-interest. Christians are concerned with *reconciliation* between conflicting parties and that goes a step further than agreement. Reconciliation demands a new relationship between people. An agreement can leave the basic relationships unchanged. Reconciliation demands the establishment of a new relationship in which both parties recognise the other's rights. It doesn't mean giving in, but a patient attempt to work together to create a situation which both parties recognise as right and just. And this is something which is never final. Because of the continuing changes in the industrial situation, there needs to be a continual effort at agreement and reconciliation.

Overheard in discussion

'In the end, perhaps industrial relations are not so much about logic as about emotion, feeling, status, power. Therefore you can only resolve the problem by becoming part of this feeling network. Is this not what the Incarnation is all about? Logically, God seeing the human situation ought to have wiped the whole thing out and started again. But in fact He became part of the network in a living way in Jesus.'

'Being a Christian in industry means being "open to the leading of the spirit". It sometimes means being "gloriously inconsistent" because this means being true to the leadership of Christ in any situation. In negotiations, for instance, you have to do your homework, of course, and use all the logic you know. You go as far as you can with facts and analysis, but you know that in the end what is going to solve it is a little bit of a miracle – the Holy Spirit if you like. For this reason, maybe prayer is as important as logic before you go to a meeting.'

CHANGE

Again, much has been said about change in industry and the appropriate attitudes to it. Change has always been a feature of industrial society but in the last few years we have become aware of an accelerating pace of change creating entirely new situations for which we have no guidelines in conventional wisdom and for which many of the existing structures are irrelevant.

I well remember a teacher of economics, who had been out of the country for the best part of a year, confessing to a group of managers and trade union officials, 'Frankly, when I come back there are so many changes, so many of the old familiar landmarks are disappearing and so much of what is going on doesn't fit in with traditional economic theories, I'm wondering if I've got anything left to teach!' It is that sort of radical change – causing the severest disorientation – which is hitting people at all levels of industry today.

Shaking foundations

Numerous attempts have been made to describe and analyse what is happening. There is the growth of industrial capability in developing nations which had previously supplied raw material to the industrial West; there is the energy crisis; resource scarcity; population increase – and, more recently, the all-pervasive effect of the microprocessor. No wonder people feel that the ground is moving under their feet and have a sense of lostness in a world which doesn't look the same any more.

The problem for the Christian Church at such a time is that when everything else is changing, people look to the Church as being the one institution that won't change! It is important, therefore, to establish the Biblical view. Jesus warned his disciples not to put their trust in human structures whether physical, legal or national. When they drew his attention to the magnificence of the buildings of the temple in Jerusalem he warned, 'There shall not be left one stone upon another.' 'Here we have no continuing city', says St. Paul; 'Behold I am making all things new' we read in Revelation; and Jesus calls for 'new wine skins for new wine'. The message is not one of a static world but of a *dynamic* world in which movement and change are going on all the time – in which forces of evil are at work, and forces of good, and in which Christians are always looking forward to 'a better country'.

We shall be suspicious, therefore, of calls to 'get back to normality' and of those whose objective is 'to settle down'. It is not exceptional for those whose lives have been shattered by redundancy, to report six months later after finding a new job, 'It was the best thing that happened to me. It has opened up a new world'. They have discovered that God is on the other side of change.

Society tested

A time of change, however, can be a time when people get hurt. In particular, it is the weak who suffer most and however much Christians recognise the will of God in change, it cannot be at the expense of the weaker brethren. 'A time of change is a time when the compassion and the corporate solidarity of a society is tested' (Clarke). Most of us can be 'sensible' about change when our lives are not involved – or when we have resources to see us through. Christians will not be satisfied, however, when the 'economic case' has been made, but will want to see that the burden of change is being fairly and equitably carried by society as a whole.

A time of change is a time of judgment for a society. A time for looking again at basic attitudes and relationships and institutions, and recognising what needs to be **changed** (the essence of repentance). We naturally shy away from the necessity of this because of the threat to our own present way of life. But Christians who have an understanding of the importance of judgment and repentance in the process of personal renewal have a responsibility to point to the relevance of these factors in the renewal of society as a whole.

Never easy

To be involved in changing society is never easy but it is the essence of repentance. It is more difficult at a time of little growth than at a time of expansion. At such a time as this all sorts of expectations will be unfulfilled and 'looking for scapegoats' will be the order of the day. It is a time when no reliable blueprints are available for the future, when palliative measures which prop up old structures are necessary in order to buy time, and when experiment with new ways has to run parallel with the continuance of old ones.

Christians need to stay with this confusion and not to get away from it too easily or too quickly. They will not under-estimate the complexity of the situation. They will recognise that the problems that face us are inter-related and that what seems to be a solution to one problem may well create bigger problems in other areas. Nevertheless, they will not be afraid to ask fundamental questions about our life-style – nor to entertain 'visions' of a better society – however provisional it may be. And remembering how God came amongst men in the village carpenter in remote Nazareth, they will not neglect to look for his renewing activity on the 'fringes' of our society.

MEANING AND PURPOSE

During the 'Fairfield's experiment' of the late '60s (when men in the Govan shipyard were invited to participate fully in the decisions of their firm), meetings were arranged from time to time between local clergy and shop stewards in the Pearce Institute, Govan. It was during one such meeting that a particularly vocal shop steward said, 'This job gives my life meaning and purpose'. He explained that he used to 'follow the wages' up and down the river and was never in the same yard for more than 3 months at a time (while the overtime lasted). But he had been in Fairfield's 18 months because he had become 'involved' in his daily work in a new way.

Whether this man is typical or not, there is plenty of evidence that to a greater or lesser degree most workers are looking for more than wages in their daily work. Wages are important – they are the basic reason for working – but more is expected. And the behavioural scientists have spent a lot of time showing how work must match *all* the needs of man and not just his need for pay. There is, of course, a debate going on as to whether work should be the only thing that gives meaning and purpose to life (as it is alleged the Protestant work ethic suggests). Whatever we may feel about that, it is certainly true that among those who have work to do, wages are not the only thing that they are looking for. 'Man does not live by bread alone'.

Rewards

But meaning and purpose seems to be what modern

industry finds it most difficult to offer its workers. And this, it is claimed, is what leads to the feeling of alienation of modern man (see previous section). What industry can offer are higher material rewards than you would get in a pre-industrial society. So it concentrates on wages, as if to say, 'It's not much of a job, but think of the rewards!' And goes on to promise ever increasing rewards, through more and more efficient methods.

Voices are being raised in the industrial community pointing to the dangers inherent in such an attitude. Among them are those (e.g. Kenneth Adams of Windsor) who point to the danger for any society where men cannot affirm the worth of their daily work. 'Any society which cannot affirm the worth of the central activity by which it lives, cannot be a healthy society' – however high may be the material rewards. And it is claimed that this has a lot to do with industry's failure to attract the best young men and women from schools and universities. They look for professions with more meaning and purpose.

Ambiguity

In a pre-industrial society, however difficult, exhausting and miserable work on the land might often be, at least men knew the worth of what they were doing; that it would bring food and life and happiness to their families and their community. It is not so easy to affirm the worth of the work in which many people are involved in a modern industrial society. Apart from the dehumanising effects of the division of labour and the methods of mass-production, there is an ambiguity about the purpose of much of our industrial activity which prevents men from being wholehearted about it.

It's not just the makers of atom bombs who find it difficult to affirm the worth of their work. It applies, for instance, to brewery workers—with a high rate of alcoholism in our society, and similarly to the tobacco manufacturers; to the car workers depending on more and more people buying cars when fossil fuels are getting dangerously scarce and pollution is a growing threat; and similarly to steel workers who provide the material for cars; even to agricultural workers today using modern farming methods which sometimes raise questions about man's stewardship of earth's resources. And behind these and many more in industry there are the bankers, the lawyers, the teachers and the trainers, whose work supports industry. In a great number of jobs in modern society men find themselves less than wholehearted about the work they are doing and unable, therefore, confidently to affirm the worth of it.

Wheat and tares

Any effort to recover again a sense of meaning and purpose in daily work must reckon with this ambiguity in men's minds. It was a banker who, on being upbraided by his minister for not attending church, said, 'You ministers just heap guilt on my head without giving me any help in carrying it'. Neither the banker nor any of the other workers mentioned above would expect the Church to give blanket approval to all the objectives and practices of industry and commerce. Nor would it be realistic to ask men to withdraw from what they cannot fully affirm. Maybe there is a need to recognise the significance of Jesus' parable of the wheat and the tares in relation to this situation and to understand the truth that in real life we have to live with the good and the bad, seldom getting the satisfaction of knowing the absolute goodness of what we are doing, but pursuing our task nevertheless, for the sake of the good in it.

If men are to live in this ambiguous situation they must accentuate the positive in their work. We must not expect every job to be 'pure' in its worth for society or its service of man. But every job has something constructive about it and the Christian will hold that element as his clear objective. At the same time he will not gloss over the unconstructive or the anti-social elements in his work. The grace of God will help him to live with them, but he will not be able to adopt an uncritical affirmation and will play his part in 'eliminating the negative'.

In most cases this will involve him in responsible participation in the development of the aims and purposes of society as a whole. It is the whole of our society that needs redemption and again we are aware of the impossibility of separating the Christian life from the process of working out the aims and objectives of our society and the ways in which these can be served by the work of men. It is here especially, amid the cynicism and despair of men, that the Christian's faith in the redemptive power of God and the Christian's sense of victory – albeit in terms of a Cross – are most needed.

Man in his strength

Perhaps a further point needs to be made. Much is

said today about the problems of industry and the media tend to dwell on them to the exclusion of its achievements. And we in the Church have tended to follow the media – especially as we are more used to dealing with man in his weakness. But in industry we meet 'man in his strength' and we should not be afraid to acknowledge this and to rejoice in it – and help men to feel God's approval. Paul says that Christ is God's YES to man. God says YES before he says NO to man. So we should not be afraid to celebrate man's achievements in industrial life. They glorify God.

Both in production – and who can fail to wonder at some of the remarkable achievements of men – and in providing relationships which enhance human life (many a young lad has had the pattern of his life set by a concerned journeyman), in providing wealth for all the worthwhile 'services' in our society and in innumerable examples of self-giving and self-sacrifice, there is much to affirm and to rejoice in in the industry of our land. Accentuating the negative can lead people to expect only the worst. Opening men's eyes to the positive and constructive in industrial life can lead to greater hope and commitment.

POWER AND AUTHORITY

In modern industry we are continually aware of the immense powers which are in the hands of some men. Physical power, of course. But also financial power, technical power, bureaucratic power, social power, national and international power. No wonder ordinary men feel very small and at the mercy of big powers over which they have no control and which may not be used in their interests. Some, of course, have a place in the power structure, either through being on a board of directors or an employers' association, or managing a bank, etc. Others, through a position in the management structure of a particular firm, exercise authority over a larger or smaller group of men.

One of the reasons for the existence of industrial mission is the feeling that the Christian Church has not taken seriously the existence of massive power centres in industrial society and their effect on individual human lives. In particular there has been a failure to recognise that power can become embedded in structures and thus retained long past the time when there is any justification for it. Paul reminds us of the 'principalities and powers...the spirit of wickedness in high places.' It is the corporate power of groups and communities and the spirit which motivates them which needs to be continually scrutinised and if necessary challenged.

Countervailing power

One effect of the exercise of such immense power in industrial life has been the growth of the countervailing power of the trade unions. The gradual development of this power, built up by the sacrifices of countless ordinary working people, has done much to make other groups in our society use their power more responsibly. It may well be that strong trade unions in Britain have saved this country from the bloody revolutions which other nations have experienced. The difficulty for Christians has been that they come into such organisations armed only with a personal ethic. And as a Church we have not been able to point to an appropriate ethic for the quite different circumstances of the relationships between two power groups.

Christians, of course, are not against power. Concentration of power in certain hands in an industrial society is inevitable and necessary. God's will is order, not anarchy – and this is for the good of man. Indeed, considering the circumstances of life for Christians in the first century it is surprising how ready Paul is to declare, 'The powers that be are ordained of God', and that men should obey them as being the agents of God (Romans 13).

Prophetic role

But another strong theme in the Bible is the prophetic role of those who serve God in challenging fearlessly the abuse of power by those who wield it (e.g. Nathan, Jeremiah, Amos, etc.). Power in the hands of any man – or group of men – which is unchallengeable and uncontrolled is dangerous for individuals and for society.

Christians therefore have a duty to be continually examining the use of power either by groups or by institutions in the light of the Kingdom of God. They will not be confused by words and high sounding ideals, but look at the reality of things. Even the best structures can be used against the interests of man and can even come to embody oppression. Equally, Christians know that even in seemingly unjust situations the ends of the Kingdom of God may be served (e.g. the relationship between Philemon and Onesimus, his slave). Nevertheless, developing structures which make sure that power is used responsibly and with due accountability is one of the ways in which God's will is served in our industrial society.

Participation

Any discussion of the responsible use of power raises the question of participation in decision-making. One of the implicit assumptions of industrialisation so far has been the right of one group of men to hire the labour of other men for work about which these men have had no say in terms of objective or practice. And whether or not this is acceptable in the short term, it is no longer acceptable as a more permanent arrangement. Part of man's God-given potential is his capacity – indeed his need – to weigh up the options of life, to make responsible decisions and to contribute to corporate goals, and the organisation of working life should allow a man the maximum possibility of doing so.

Our of all that has been written and said about participation perhaps two statements may provide some further insights, one from an industrial mission conference and the other from a manager who has gone further than most in introducing participation.

(a) 'Participation includes a sharing or giving and taking, including a sharing of power that is non-manipulative. Participation is a means and not an end. Participation should be introduced participatively. Participation should be tested by creative fruits – there should be hard evidence of change. Participation should be trust-creating.'

(b) 'When you genuinely want to give something away, it's then that you hit trouble with the workforce. If, on the other hand, you say you're in difficulties, they often respond. You see, when you are offering something to workers, they have no part in the decision. Power remains with you. When you come and admit you're in difficulties and appeal for help, you're placing yourself on the same level and inviting them to take part in joint decisions. It's power-sharing in action.'

Not starry-eyed

While expressing concern for maximum participation in industry, Christians will not be 'starry-eyed' about the inevitable 'success' of giving people a greater say in the running of their own affairs. The need for participation does not exclude the need for structures and disciplines within which men must work. The Biblical view of man is two-fold. On the one hand man is made in the image of God with great potential – and great responsibility. On the other hand, man is prone to sin, self-interest and the misuse of his freedom which can affect the lives of others. For this reason men, from the shopfloor to the boardroom, need a structure for their working life where discipline is firm but fair.

And while talking about discipline, Christians see the purpose of it as being towards the promotion of repentance and renewal rather than judgement and condemnation. To ignore a man's faults may save embarrassment, but in fact it is telling him that you don't think he can do any better. To subject him to agreed discipline is often the most convincing way of letting him know that you have far higher expectations of him – that you believe in him and in his potential.

The servant manager

For those who have the personal responsibility of bearing authority among their fellows it is important that they see it as a task to be fulfilled on behalf of the group as a whole. Jesus contrasts the attitude of the leaders of the Gentiles who 'Lord it' over their people with his own attitude, 'I am among you as he that serveth'. Thus he gives us a new understanding of leadership and of authority-bearing. It is given for the service of those among whom it is exercised. The manager is the servant. He holds his power for others. With a more general acceptance of this interpretation of the purpose and use of authority there might be fewer who would refuse to follow Paul's injunction to 'pray for those in authority over us'!

COMMUNITY

In a sense all sections of this report so far have been about community. But maybe there is a need for a brief word to point directly to the desperate need in our industrial society for the recovery of a true sense of community.

One of the unwelcome consequences of the development of industrialisation has been the steady erosion of the traditional bonds that hold a community together. 'There are too few things the British people can affirm together these days', said someone in a group recently. This becomes more evident the more interdependent our society becomes – especially when an increasing number of groups fail to have their expectations fulfilled.

Class divisions

Some would describe this breakdown in community in Marxist terms, pointing to the underlying class divisions which our industrial system has produced and which it seeks to preserve. Anyone looking seriously at the factors which militate against community in British society could not ignore 'class' (however you like to define it). And for all our talk about creating community, the Christian Church has generally been slow to recognise the significance of 'class' in determining attitudes and behaviour. I remember asking a very worthy shop steward convener (a member of the Kirk) why he didn't attend services more often. His answer was: 'All week I have to work for a hard manager and often to struggle with him on behalf of the men. When I come to church on Sunday, who is up there taking the collection but the same manager. I have to work for him during the week. But he and his like seem to be in charge on Sunday too.'

The pity is that concern about class divisions has been left to Communists. The fact that they see *everything* in terms of class and press it to extremes, should not blind Christians to the need to be actively working for the abolition of those things which create class division.

Strangers

Apart, however, from 'class', another important factor, militating against community in our industrial society, is the increasing specialisation in working life. People in one occupation have less and less idea about what the other man's work entails. Few people outside mining areas really know what a miner's life is like. And the same applies to hospital porters, investment managers, teachers, railwaymen, computer programmers, firemen and so on. We've become 'strangers' to each other and increasingly feel misunderstood by the rest of society. As a result we see each other as a threat rather than belonging together.

One of the great texts of the Bible is, 'I was a stranger and ye took me in'. Fear of the stranger is one of the fundamental causes of the breakdown of community and Christians have a role to play in holding groups in industry together to listen and to think along with each other so that they no longer see each other as strangers to be feared, but as fellow human beings who have needs and concerns like their own. This isn't to gloss over differences of opinion. It is to give a better chance of finding a common mind and a basis for true community. Jesus showed that in relationships between Roman and Jew, master and slave, the Kingdom can be an immediate reality. But within such situations Christians, by the attitudes they adopt, inevitably become the agents of change.

Not individualistic

Finally in this connection it is not without

significance that Jesus came talking about a 'Kingdom' – risking all the misunderstandings and false expectations which might be aroused by the use of that word. In choosing the 'Kingdom of God' as the centrepiece of his Gospel, he countersigned man's longing for true community. He was concerned about people as persons, but salvation was not individualistic. The joy of the Gospel was not personal moral rectitude. It was to be found in community, in the Kingdom.

So Christians must be prepared to continue talking with men about our society in all its forms, exploring with them the nature of the Kingdom in relation to it.

Part III

Some Thoughts on
Presenting the Gospel Today

'Industrial Mission is a Christian presence in the
industrial world. It involves taking part in the
conversations which occur there, being sensitive
to what is happening, and seeking to understand.
Through this process of participation, reflection
and evaluation, industrial mission works for the
embodiment of Christian values in the
relationships, methods and goals of industry and
commerce.' (B.C.C. Report)

This aim – to take part in the on-going discussion
within industry – means that we are not always
trying to force discussion on to 'religious' lines and
that there are few formal occasions when industrial
chaplains make a 'statement of the faith' to people
in industry. It doesn't mean that the Faith – or a
particular feature of it – is not discussed. Sometimes
men ask the sort of searching questions you would
get elsewhere – and chaplains will do their best to
answer them. But mostly questions about the
meaning of the Gospel are related to industrial
situations.

Two-way process
We have also become acutely aware that the
communication of the Faith is a two-way process
and can be a very costly experience. As one
chaplain put it, 'The Gospel is not just something I

have to tell others. It is something that happens
between people. It is very costly to be involved in
this experience. Each time I share with another a
Gospel truth, it judges me also. I must be prepared
to place my own prejudices, class outlook, dogmas
and dearly held opinions under the scrutiny of
Christ. A little bit of me has to die every time I
engage in evangelism.'

A statement from the French Reformed Church
also emphasises the importance of 'sharing' in
evangelism. 'Evangelisation means the transition
from a joy discovered to a joy shared. It fulfils itself
not in self-affirmation but in a free interchange of
ideas, which keeps the Christian always humble. In
this it is completely different from proselytism,
which stems from a spirit of mastery and from rigid
ideas of truth to which men must submit, a spirit
which refuses to recognise in its neighbour a man of
free and original mind.'

Who says it?

In thinking about any form of evangelism, we would
also want to heed the warning from the Hong Kong
Industrial Mission Team given in the first of its 'Ten
Theses on Labour Evangelism'. It declares, 'For
Labour Evangelism, the trustworthiness of the
Christian message depends on the trustworthiness of
the evangelist.' In explanation it goes on to say,
'The communication of the Christian message
requires trust. For workers in general trust does not
so much come from what is being said as from who
says it. We once heard a preacher invited by the
factory manager, tell the shop-floor workers over a
loud speaker that 'Man does not live by bread

alone.' It was plain that workers thought he was talking nonsense. Worker reaction to his message ranged from apathy to resentment to outright hatred. Yet the same quotation from an industrial missioner found warm acceptance: 'Right, poor as we are, money is not everything.' The Gospel must be communicated by an evangelist whom workers trust or there will be serious distortion.

The importance of this warning is hard to over-emphasise. It is something which is too often ignored in the Church's evangelistic efforts. It is certainly crucial for industrial mission. As Dr. Horace Walker said to industrial chaplains some years ago, 'It's not a question of whether what you say is right, but of whether you have the right to say it.'

Establishing trust takes time. Industrial chaplains in particular have to work hard at becoming the sort of people whom workers will genuinely be able to trust. In some respects the chaplain will always remain an outsider and in the end of the day the agents for the communication of the Gospel in industry will be Christian laymen who work there – hence the importance of seeing that they have the resources and support they need for that task.

Confidence

A further point needs to be made about our stance in respect to the communication of the Gospel and this relates to our confidence in what we have to share with others. The fact that we reject the shallowness and inadequacy of triumphalism should not prevent us from displaying confidence in the message of Jesus for men today. Laymen in this respect have normally much to teach the clergy.

When a chaplain in one group referred to the 'Communist challenge', two of the members (a manager and a trade unionist) said that such talk was out of date. They both had daily dealings with Communists and felt that over the years it was Christians who influenced Communists rather than the other way about. 'If you're thinking about "the Communist challenge"', said the manager, 'you're probably really concerned about preserving the status quo.' But that's not good Christian thinking. It is we who should be challenging Communism with a more humane ethic.'

Groundwork

With these provisos – and warnings – have we then any insights as to 'how to present the Gospel to people outside the Church'. Not nearly as many as we might be expected to have after all these years – though maybe some of what has already been stated in Part II would be relevant here. In terms of the parable of the sower, we've spent a lot of time analysing the soil, feeding the ground and doing some ploughing. We're still far from understanding what sort of seed will 'do well' in the industrial ground of today. It is my impression, however, that our work does create some genuine interest in the Christian answer and that sufficient trust has been generated to allow us to be more direct in our approach.

Each chaplain would deal with this differently. I would like to mention briefly two points which I believe ought to be remembered in such an approach.

CHALLENGING ASSUMPTIONS

There is a clear need to challenge some of the assumptions which are so easily and unthinkingly accepted today.

Idols

What has already been said about the idols which men worship is relevant here. The fact that the Christian God has been removed from the market place does not mean that worship of the gods has ceased in that arena. The issue is not for or against God, but 'which god'? The worshipper is not unaffected by the object he worships and therefore since we are all involved in this business of worship, it is of importance to us to know whether or not we are worshipping false gods.

Faith

There is also a prevalent assumption that the whole notion of 'faith' is obsolete. Normally, when you mention the word, people feel that you have left the world of reality and disappeared through a spiritual escape-hatch. They need to be reminded that faith plays a significant part in everyone's daily life and that it's quite false to divide those who 'live by faith' from those who need no such 'crutch'!

Anyone in regular contact with men in industry must be impressed by the toucing faith people have that in our industrial society, life must get better all the time. We have more or less ironed out all the problems (bad harvests, droughts, diseases, etc.) which might hold back the rate of advance – and if there isn't continuous growth, it must be someone's fault. The Biblical word is much more realistic and gives no such guarantee either for personal or corporate life. It does call on people to stand together in bad times as in good; to rejoice in the bounties of the earth but not to assume them as a right.

Or again, the Marxist puts his *faith* in Marx's interpretation of history and his consequent analysis of present and future social change. He believes Marx's 'prophecy' about the inevitability of the coming revolution and the blessings of the classless society. His faith is strong enough for him to work and to sacrifice for it.

Ignazio Silone, the Italian Communist leader who finally broke with the Communist party in the Stalin era, claimed that he did so because of a '*recovery of faith*' in the things that had first sent him into the Socialist movement. 'I do not conceive Socialist policy as tied to any particular theory', he said, 'but to a faith. The more socialist theories claim to be scientific, the more transitory they are; but socialist values are permanent. The distinction between theories and values is not sufficiently recognised, but it is fundamental. On a group of theories one can found a school, but on a group of values one can found a culture, a civilisation, a new way of living together among men.'

Values

Mention of values reminds us of another assumption on the part of people today, namely that we shall automatically continue to enjoy the values of a Christian society (and improve on them) long after the disappearance of the faith that inspired them. We talk confidently about a 'pluralist society' as if it was a better guarantee of a free and caring community than a Christian one.

We certainly do have to live in a pluralist society but that should make us all the more concerned about how the values we cherish are to be maintained and advanced among us. The evidence of the world and of history is not that this comes naturally or that all men recognise the worth of them. The question must be faced: 'Where do values come from?' And at this point – as Dr. Ramsey would say – 'the person of Jesus Christ may legitimately be brought on to the scene'. Even the atheistic Nietzsche admitted that in Jesus, 'A revaluation of all values is announced here.'

CENTRALITY OF JESUS

So it seems to me that we should concentrate on Jesus and the centrality of Jesus in the Christian message. There is still an enormous respect for Jesus among men and women at all levels of industry. They may be critical of the Church, or the clergy, or elders or members. But not of Jesus. His unique place in human history is recognised on all sides. It was the Czech Marxist philosopher, Milan Machovec, who drew the attention of his fellows to the remarkable fact that 'critics practically never reproach Christians for being followers of Christ, but on the contrary for not being such, for betraying the cause of Jesus.'

E

But how do we re-awaken the dormant feelings of respect men have for Jesus and how make real his presence in human life today? Here especially we must take heed of the warnings at the beginning of this section about 'costly sharing' and about 'building up trust' and not rush arrogantly to 'win' men. Hopefully some of the points made in the second part of this report about the relationship of Jesus and his teaching to specific industrial situations will prove useful.

Three points

I would like, however, to make three points in this connection which it seems to me should guide our approach and I would like to illustrate them by questions from Hans Kung: 'On being a Christian'.

Firstly, *Jesus himself is the message.* The integrity of Jesus' life is crucial to the content of his message. No Marxist would claim that Marxism depends on the matching of Marx's life with his teaching. No Freudian would make such a claim either. But Jesus is the 'living embodiment of his cause'. 'Christians are ultimately dependent on this person, not only on his teaching, but also on his life, death and new life. As a concrete historical person Jesus possesses an impressiveness which is missing from an eternal idea, a universal norm, a conceptual system'. (Kung).

Secondly, therefore, we should be content to spend a lot of time *talking with men about the human being Jesus* – a man among men. It seems to me that the premature emphasis on the divine in Jesus has distanced him unnecessarily from ordinary people and that we cannot expect men to find the

Son of God until they have really met the man
Jesus. To say this is no more than to underline
God's intention in the incarnation. Here again
Kung distinguishes between 'exaltation Christology'
– beginning with Jesus the man and in him
recognising God – and 'incarnational Christology'
which sees Jesus firstly as the pre-existent Son of
God who came down to earth to become man. He
claims that the former is truer to the original
Christian proclamation.

Thirdly, as with the first evangelists we will have
to *concentrate on the death of Jesus* as being the
place where clues to the ultimate truth about life are
to be found. It was William Temple who said that
life is not to be thought of as a picture in which all
the parts exist at once. Rather it is like a drama
where – if it is good enough – the full meaning of
the first scene only becomes apparent with the final
curtain. So it is with the life of Jesus. It has
meaning for us only as we have reckoned with his
death and resurrection.

Hans Kung heightens the significance of Jesus'
death by comparing it with the deaths of other
great religious leaders:

'Moses, Buddha, Confucius, all died at a ripe old
age, successful despite many disappointments, in
the midst of their disciples and supporters....

Moses died in sight of the promised land, in
the midst of his people, at the age of 120 years...

Buddha died at the age of eighty, peacefully,
his disciples around him....

Confucius returned in old age to Lu – after he
had spent his last years in training a group of

mainly noble disciples, to preserve and continue his work . . . .

Muhammad, after he had thoroughly enjoyed the last years of his life as political ruler of Arabia, died in the midst of his harem in the arms of his favorite wife.

'Here on the other hand we have a young man of thirty, after three years at most of activity, perhaps only a few months. Expelled from society, betrayed and denied by his disciples and supporters, mocked and ridiculed by his opponents, forsaken by men and even by God, he goes through a ritual death.'

The question with which we are confronted is why, after such an ignominious death, deserted by his terrified disciples, Jesus became the main content of their proclamation, not in spite of his death, but precisely *because of it*.

It is on their response to this question that men in any generation and in any circumstances find meaning and hope in the Christian Faith and we should expect it to be no different today.

It may not be that traditional formulations of doctrine are helpful to contemporary man and in particular we must be prepared to look afresh at the death and resurrection of Jesus in relation to man's daily work experience. Such exploration frequently reveals a deeper understanding of the meaning of the Cross than is to be found in the most prestigious doctrinal statements. As an illustration of such exploration I would like to quote in conclusion an experience of Horst Symanowski, one of the leaders of industrial mission in Germany, which he related at a conference in Baird Hall, Glasgow, some years ago.

The bamboo stick

He explained that a group of workers from a local factory came to his house every week to talk about their working life and he got them to look at the Bible in relation to it (on the pretext that they would help him in his preparation for his Sunday sermon!). One member of the group was a man of much common sense (though he was no church-goer). He was held in great respect by the others and they tried to persuade him to stand for the works council. He resisted this suggestion, claiming that he would just be taking on a 'load of worry' and that 'that's the quickest way to lose friends'. However, he was persuaded that it was his 'duty', so he accepted nomination and was duly elected.

It was three months before Symanowski met him again. 'It's just as I thought,' he said. 'I'm now in a world of half-truths and double-talk and of people concerned only for themselves. I've lost many good friends and don't seem to have achieved anything. You know, if you twist a bamboo stock one way with one hand and the other way with the other hand, it splits in the middle. That's the position I'm in, management twisting one way and workers the other – and it's all because of your damn Bible'.

'You know, that's what the Bible is all about', said Symanowski. 'What do you mean?' asked the man. 'Well, right at the centre of the Bible there's a man who knew all about half-truths and double-talk – all about rejection and desertion by his friends – all about the bamboo stick, though he knew it as a

Cross. But that's where Christians believe life began. He didn't give up. He believed that whatever the appearances, the final word lay with God, and because of his faith he gave life to the world. This is where life can begin for you – if you're willing to let him share your bamboo stick.'

Everyone present at Baird Hall recognised the authenticity of the situation this man was in – and also the truth of 'what the Bible is all about'. And I'm still amazed at the number of people who, on hearing the story, come up to me afterwards and say, 'You know, that's *my* situation too. How true!' At least they've begun to recognise the significance of Jesus' death for their lives. And in most cases I'm sure they've been encouraged to go on with a bit more hope because in some way they're sharing their life experience with him.

POSTSCRIPT

No good evangelist would make a statement of the Faith without inviting his hearers to do something about it – to 'come and join us'. This is part of the message too. *Jesus is the centre of a movement in human life rather than the object of doctrinal statements.* To be a disciple of his is to be part of his movement in the world and to work for his objectives.

So the proclamation of the Gospel must be associated with the life of a Christian community. And perhaps our confusion in industrial mission lies in our lack of confidence in the official Christian community (the Church) and our failure to develop any group within it in which men would experience the community of Christ.

I can only state that this is a question which deeply concerns us in industrial mission. We ourselves have been greatly enriched by our own experience of the fellowship of Christ's Church. But we would be less than honest if we pretended that the image of our Church today is a missionary asset among people in industry. I personally believe this to be a crucial issue for the future. As Dr. C. E. Raven said 30 years ago in a discussion on industrial mission, 'When you've made contact with men in industry and begun to talk with them about the Faith, you've only done half the job. You've still got to make our Churches places where men with an alien background will find the support and inspiration of a true Christian Community.'

Appendix 1

Biblical View of Work

(A Paper prepared for Education Committee, 1974)

Work is accepted *in the Bible* as a natural part of human life. God has ordained that man should live by working for his daily bread.

Work is also described in terms of man's co-operation with God in the continuing work of creation. It is part of the image of God in man that he is given this creative role by God.

There is also included in this the idea of the stewardship of the earth and of natural resources. Man is 'to tend and to keep it'.

Man without work is not the being God intended him to be. In a sense, therefore, man has a 'right to work', as well as a responsibility for work.

The Bible recognises that work is hard, sometimes monotonous and exhausting. It is overshadowed by man's sin and his rejection of God's partnership and his laws. Man's work is often therefore frustrating, and brings forth 'thorns and thistles'.

In the New Testament work is seen as a wholesome thing (in contrast with the Greek view). 'The workman is worthy of his hire'. 'He who does not work neither shall he eat'. Paul calls on servants to obey their masters not as men pleasers but as if they were working for God. Obedience in work is not something which necessarily reduces a man's dignity. It depends on whether a man in his work is serving larger ends—in the case of a Christian, the purposes of God. However imperfect working life may be, this is the way people are fed and clothed, and that is God's will.

Work in Western industrial society has, to a remarkable degree, fulfilled God's will to feed the hungry and clothe the naked. There are also clear signs of the fulfilment of God's purposes in the development of industry and technology. Man's creativity and ingenuity have brought many blessings to the world.

The danger is that man in pride forgets his partnership with God. Good husbandry and stewardship are transformed by the demands of ever-increasing consumption, and work becomes a thoughtless exploitation of the earth's limited resources. There must be a large question-mark over the purpose of work in our society.

Christians believe that all life is redeemed by Christ, and their calling is to be His agents in working life.

(a) In person-to-person relationships. As God became part of the human network in Jesus, so the work of redemption must go on today in person-to-person relationships wherever Christians find themselves in working life. Industry provides a network of a kind, and Christians need to learn how to use it.

(b) Because of the large-scale organisation of industry and the concentration of powers which affect the lives of men, for good or ill, the fulfilment of God's will requires participation by Christians in the groups and institutions of industrial life.

This requires patience and persistence but Christians have much to contribute and it is through the work of the leaven within the industrial community that Jesus chooses to pursue his work of redemption rather than through the dramatic act from outside.

Appendix 2

Weber: The Protestant Ethic and the Spirit of Capitalism

(A Paper prepared for Society, Religion and Technology Project, 1976)

Weber is not trying to show that Protestantism 'caused' capitalism. He is talking about the psychological climate in which capitalism arose. 'The tonic which braced the new bourgeoisie for the conflict was a new concept of religion – the pursuit of wealth is not merely an advantage, it is a duty.' This led to a change in moral standards and converted a natural frailty into an ornament of the spirit. 'Capitalism', he claimed, 'was the social counterpart of Calvinist theology.'

One of the central doctrines of *Calvinism* is *predestination.* This doctrine asserts that God has fore-ordained some men to salvation and the rest to damnation. The agonising question for the Calvinist was therefore, 'Am I among the elect or the damned?' How could he tell? Calvin, with cold consistency, said he couldn't, only God knew. But later Calvinists said he might tell 'by seeing if there is any evidence of your faith in your conduct', i.e. conduct which served the glory of God. Good works were, of course, useless in attaining salvation (that was important Reformation doctrine). But good works are indispensable as a sign of election.

Thus, what had been put out the front door got back in, in a more virulent form, by the back door.

Further, the Calvinists claimed that it is only *activity* that serves the Glory of God – not leisure or laxity, idleness or enjoyment. Baxter preaches continuous hard bodily or mental labour. 'Work hard at your calling'; it saves you from the temptations of the world.

This word *'calling'* is important for Weber's case. For *Catholics* it usually referred to those who felt a calling to a 'religious' life, in a monastery for instance. There were, of course, the ordinary men and women from whom no specially virtuous behaviour was to be expected. They would need the Sacraments of the Church regularly to get salvation (and probably stay a good time in Purgatory). But monks and nuns had a special 'calling' to a life of spiritual asceticism and virtue. Their reward was not in this world but in the world to come.

For *Luther* a man's 'calling' referred to life in the world, but 'in the station in life into which he had been born'. It was in fulfilling his duty there that he would glorify God. For *Calvin* a man's 'calling' was 'a strenuous enterprise chosen by himself and to be pursued with a sense of religious responsibility'. A man's calling was something he would move towards – out beyond his present position.

Weber claims that neither Catholicism nor Lutheranism was a suitable ground for capitalism. But Calvinism was eminently suitable. Having rejected the idea that the perfect life could only be found by turning one's back on the world, Calvin had to work out a totally new system of life for men. It had to be something to be worked out with the same concern as the monk for the glory of God, but this time in the ordinary business of the world. 'Godly discipline' was its mark and the virtues of the elect were diligence, thrift, sobriety, prudence – all the virtues which in the business world are a reliable passport to prosperity. Labour itself became not just a means but a spiritual end. Covetousness was less to be feared than sloth. The fulfilment of one's duty in worldly affairs is the highest form of moral activity.

Thus Weber builds his case. Throw in a Biblical reference to the parable of the talents (taken in a literalistic form) and you are almost explicitly saying that the man who doesn't make the wealth which God has given him, produce more wealth (to the glory of God of course), is not fulfilling God's will. And that, Weber claims, is to provide a moral basis for capitalism.

Note: (a) Weber makes a distinction between 'speculative and adventurous capitalism' on the one hand (which he identifies with Jews) and Protestant rational organisation of capital and labour to the glory of God on the other. There had always been adventurers ready to take a risk on a venture in the hope of quick gain. But moden capitalism was a systematic, rational, responsible organisation. It was an on-going, continuous structure for industry and society. Calvin, of course, believed that to glorify God there must be strict control over the purposes of economic enterprise – it must be for the social good.

(b) Weber also notes the difference between the Catholic and the Protestant attitudes to usury. Acquisition of wealth for its own sake had never been fully accepted by the pre-Reformation Church. But Protestants were faced with the urgent question what to do with the wealth which their labour brought them. Their ascetic living standards prevented them from consuming it all themselves and they must therefore use it for the social good – which meant creating more wealth. (There is a hint of a difference between taking interest on a loan to a friend in distress and putting together some capital with others, the better to use your labour – and benefit everyone).

(c) Protestantism condemned dishonesty and impulsive avarice. It also condemned the pursuit of riches 'for its own sake'. But once riches had come it was a sin not to use them to the glory of God – the creation of more wealth.

(It is interesting to note that the wealth of the Protestant capitalist owed much to limitation of his personal consumption and much also to his ability to increase other people's appetite for consumption.)

Note: Essential to the organisation of capitalism was the existence of free-labour available for organisation. Previously the employer (the lord) was bound in contract with worker (serf) to give him work. With the freeing of men, employers could take on and lay-off men as they needed them. A labour pool of free men was essential to the rise of capitalism.